"This generation of Christians inhabit cultures that sometimes reject not only biblical revelation about reality, but also the reality of reality itself. The Questions for Restless Minds series poses many of the toughest questions faced by young Christians to some of the world's foremost Christian thinkers and leaders. Along the way, this series seeks to help the Christian next generation to learn how to think biblically when they face questions in years to come that perhaps no one yet sees coming."

—Russell Moore,
public theologian, *Christianity Today*

"If you're hungry to go deeper in your faith, wrestle with hard questions, and are dissatisfied with the shallow content on your social media newsfeed, you'll really appreciate this series of thoughtful deep dives on critically important topics like faith, the Bible, friendship, sexuality, philosophy, and more. As you engage with some world-class Christian scholars, you'll be encouraged, equipped, challenged, and above all invited to love God more with your heart, soul, mind, and strength."

—Andy Kim,
multiethnic resource director, InterVarsity Christian Fellowship

T0334952

What Is a Christian Worldview?

Questions for Restless Minds

Questions for Restless Minds

QUESTIONS FOR RESTLESS MINDS

What Is a Christian Worldview?

Graham A. Cole

D. A. Carson,
Series Editor

LEXHAM PRESS

What Is a Christian Worldview?
Questions for Restless Minds, edited by D. A. Carson

Lexham Press, 1313 Commercial St., Bellingham, WA 98225
LexhamPress.com

Print ISBN 9781683595335
Digital ISBN 9781683595342
Library of Congress Control Number 2021937699

Lexham Editorial: Todd Hains, Abigail Stocker, Jessi Strong, Mandi Newell
Cover Design: Brittany Schrock
Interior Design: Abigail Stocker
Typesetting: ProjectLuz.com

24 iii / US

The Christ on Campus Initiative exists to inspire students on college and university campuses to think wisely, act with conviction, and become more Christlike by providing relevant and excellent evangelical resources on contemporary issues.

Visit christoncampuscci.org.

Contents

Series Preface

D. A. CARSON, SERIES EDITOR

T HE ORIGIN OF this series of books lies with a group of faculty from Trinity Evangelical Divinity School (TEDS), under the leadership of Scott Manetsch. We wanted to address topics faced by today's undergraduates, especially those from Christian homes and churches.

If you are one such student, you already know what we have in mind. You know that most churches, however encouraging they may be, are not equipped to prepare you for what you will face when you enroll at university.

It's not as if you've never known any winsome atheists before going to college; it's not as if you've never thought about Islam, or the credibility of the New Testament documents, or the nature of friendship, or gender identity, or how the claims of Jesus sound too exclusive and rather narrow, or the nature of evil. But up until now you've probably thought about such things within the shielding cocoon of a community of faith.

Now you are at college, and the communities in which you are embedded often find Christian perspectives to be at best oddly quaint and old-fashioned, if not repulsive. To use the current jargon, it's easy to become socialized into a new community, a new world.

How shall you respond? You could, of course, withdraw a little: just buckle down and study computer science or Roman history (or whatever your subject is) and refuse to engage with others. Or you could throw over your Christian heritage as something that belongs to your immature years and buy into the cultural package that surrounds you. Or—and this is what we hope you will do—you could become better informed.

But how shall you go about this? On any disputed topic, you do not have the time, and probably not the interest, to bury yourself in a couple of dozen volumes written by experts for experts. And if you did, that would be on *one* topic—and there are scores of topics that will grab the attention of the inquisitive student. On the other hand, brief pamphlets with predictable answers couched in safe slogans will prove to be neither attractive nor convincing.

So we have adopted a middle course. We have written short books pitched at undergraduates who want arguments that are accessible and stimulating, but invariably courteous. The material is comprehensive enough that it has become an important resource for pastors and other campus leaders who devote their energies to work with students. Each book ends with a brief annotated bibliography and study questions, intended for readers who want to probe a little further.

Lexham Press is making this series available as attractive print books and in digital formats (ebook and Logos resource). We hope and pray you will find them helpful and convincing.

1

INTRODUCTION

He took the blade. It was bright silver. He loved the way it glistened. It felt good in his hand. He cut deep into her chest again and again. He showed no emotion, no recognition of her humanity. She lay motionless, her life gone. He made no attempt to cover the body. Later that night over a beer he openly talked to a stranger in the bar about what he had done. The stranger felt ill.

W HAT ARE WE to make of this? Should someone have called 911? Should he have been arrested? Is this a Hannibal Lecter story? It all depends. To make sense of it, this narrative fragment needs placing in a larger picture or frame of reference. We need to know more.

Now suppose I were to inform you that the setting earlier that night was a back alley late at night and that the woman had been alive but drunk when she entered it, then you would be entitled to think that this is a case for CSI. The man listening to the story in the bar ought to have called the police. However, if I were to say that instead of the alley, the setting earlier that night had been a CSI autopsy room, then the complexion of the event changes your reading of it. The man with the knife is no serial killer but instead a forensic scientist. Maybe he shouldn't have talked about the details to a stranger over a beer. But if that was misconduct it was unprofessional, not criminal.

Frames of reference are keys to understanding, to reading the world of our experience. Eric Fromm found that out as a young man before he became a prominent therapist and humanist thinker. He contemplated the carnage of World War I and wondered, "How come such violence? How could cultured peoples slaughter each other in the millions?"[1] That thought led him to study Karl Marx and the outer world of human history. He wanted to make some kind of sense of the world of his experience. He also knew a young woman who committed suicide at the grave of her father. She was very beautiful and refined. "How come?" he asked. On the surface she had so much to live for. How could some kind of sense be made of it? That tragic story led him to study Sigmund Freud and the inner world of the human psyche. He found that he needed a frame of reference in which to place such events, great and small, in order to make some sense of them.

The need for a frame of reference is all the more urgent given the "meteoric shower of facts" that pour on us (to use Neil Postman's borrowed phrase). Postman quotes the poet Edna St. Vincent Millay to good effect:

Upon this gifted age, in its dark hour
Rains from the sky *a meteoric shower*
Of facts ... they lie unquestioned, uncombined.

Wisdom enough to leech us of our ill
Is daily spun, but there exists no loom
To weave it into fabric.[2]

If the fabric is to be woven, Postman argues, we need a "god" in the sense of a "grand narrative" (this is an odd use of the word "god," I might add)—one that "tells of origins and envisions a future." It must be some story "that it is possible to organize one's life around."[3] And, I might add, it must help us cope with the "meteoric shower / Of facts."

Our frame of reference matters. We all have at least one, or maybe bits of different ones that we have never been able to connect up into some sort of coherent whole. Perhaps this is a question to which we have not really turned our minds in a sustained way. If we do then the real question becomes: where do we find a frame of reference or a worldview that tells a coherent and consistent story that really understands us and illuminates the actual world in which we live? We need—if we want to be thoughtful about it—a frame of reference that is thinkable, that is, one that is not riddled with self-contradiction. It also needs to be livable—that is, we can actually live as though this frame of reference really does correspond to the world of our experience, so that we do not have to pretend that it does. (More about those criteria at a later stage.) That is not to say, however, that there may not be puzzles and mysteries left unresolved. As Moses said in ancient times, there are secret things that belong to the Lord (Deut 29:29).

Having said all that, though, a word is needed about the tricky term "worldview."[4] How does it relate to the expression I prefer, which is "frame of reference"?

2

QUESTIONING
THE QUESTION

C. E. M. Joad made a name on British radio as a brain. He was a professional philosopher at the University of London and was on a BBC radio panel called "The Brains Trust." Listeners supplied the questions. The panel would try to answer them and entertain at the same time. Invariably Professor Joad would start an answer to a question with "It all depends on what you mean by … ."[5] He became famous for it. He was right to ask questions of the question, whether the question was stated or implied. So should we. For some, worldview is a term that covers a set of answers to questions about who we are, where we have come from, why we go wrong and what we may hope for as far as change for the better is concerned. I like to call this an existential worldview because it centers on real questions about my actual existence. This understanding of worldview and my frame of reference are synonymous.

For others, worldview is a grand project of human reason that aims in a logical and coherent way to account for all that comes before human consciousness, ranging from math to economics to physics and all points in between. I call this grand project the quest for an encyclopedic worldview. Some of the biggest names in Western thought have attempted this enterprise: for example,

Plato, Aristotle, Kant, and Hegel. In fact it was Kant who coined the term worldview (German *Weltanschauung*).[6] Put another way, this ambitious project attempts to write a book of knowledge that encompasses all there is.

About this quest I have my doubts—unless, that is, the quest is shaped by an appropriate humility. Without such an attitude, there really is something valid in the postmodern criticism—Jean-François Lyotard's "incredulity towards metanarratives" comes to mind—that big picture thinking can become an expression of arrogance and a set of ideas by which to marginalize others.[7] Cold War Marxism is a case in point, as the 2006 Academy Award winning film "The Lives of Others" shows. The film sets its story in East Germany in the years just prior to and after the collapse of the Berlin Wall (1989) and brilliantly depicts the brutalizing effects of an ideology that shows utter contempt for human value.

So when I mention worldview in this piece I am not talking about the encyclopedic worldview project, which is like a frame of reference on steroids.

A TOUCHSTONE PROPOSITION

What seems to be true of a frame of reference or of both sorts of worldview, whether existential or encyclopedic, is that some proposition or claim lies at the heart of them. One philosopher, William H. Halverson, has described such a proposition—whether that proposition is implicit or explicit—as a touchstone proposition.[8] Examples are not hard to find. At the core of naturalism, for instance, is the idea that matter is all there is, while theism claims that there is a wise and good Creator. According to Halverson, this divide between naturalistic and non-naturalistic worldviews is the fundamental one. He contends:

> It may be helpful to bear in mind from the beginning, however, that one theme that underlies nearly all philosophical discussion is the perpetual conflict between *naturalistic* and *nonnaturalistic* world views. A *naturalistic* world view is one in which it is affirmed that (a) there is only one order of reality, (b) this one order of reality consists entirely of objects and events occurring in space and time, and (c) this one order of reality is completely self-dependent and self-operating. … Any world view that denies any of the above-stated tenets of naturalism, then, may be termed *nonnaturalistic*.[9]

Other examples include nihilism, which has at its heart the notion that nothing matters. Islam provides one more instance with its claim that Allah alone is God and that Muhammad is his prophet.

But what exactly is a touchstone? A touchstone is a piece of quartz that can be rubbed against what is claimed to be gold. The chemical reaction that follows will show whether the specimen of ore is real gold or fool's gold. The touchstone proposition acts as a gatekeeper to the house of knowledge—or so it is hoped. What we count as knowledge

13

has to pass the quality control of the touchstone proposition. Of course, and here's the rub, our chosen touchstone may be astray with the result that we are really in the dark but do not know it. John Warwick Montgomery tells an instructive story that makes the point.

> Once upon a time there was man who thought he was dead. His concerned wife and friends sent him to the friendly neighborhood psychiatrist. The psychiatrist determined to cure him by convincing him of one fact that contradicted his belief that he was dead. The fact that the psychiatrist settled on was the simple truth that dead men do not bleed, and he put him to work reading medical texts, observing autopsies, etc. After weeks of effort, the patient finally said, "All right! You've convinced me. Dead men do not bleed." Whereupon the psychiatrist struck him in the arm with a needle, and the blood flowed. The man looked with a contorted, ashen face and cried: "Good Lord! Dead men bleed after all!"[10]

The wrong touchstone proposition or presupposition, "I am dead!", can keep us from reality. Put another way, some frames of reference may leave us puzzled, like the young man I met some years ago. He had a real interest in history. So he studied all the evidence he could for the claim that Christ was raised from the dead. He read a book by the journalist Frank Morison.[11] Morison started off his project as an agnostic but ended as a believer in the resurrection.

Having read Morrison's *Who Moved The Stone?*, he concluded that Jesus had indeed come back from the dead. But he did not believe in the possibility of life after death for anyone else. I asked him, "How come?" He replied that he also believed in a chance universe in which freaky things could happen like a one-off resurrection.

In relation to our question "Has Christianity a worldview or frame of reference?" we need then to look for a touchstone proposition, or better still, a cluster of such, at its heart—but with this proviso. It may turn out that Christianity has a frame of reference or a worldview in the existential sense, but isn't one *itself.* It may turn out that Christianity intellectually considered in the first instance is not a worldview, but the interpretation of a slice of human history and with it a claim that the ultimate destiny of us all hangs on what happened in that history and our response to it.[12]

PASCAL'S *PENSÉE* NO. 12

One thing a frame of reference must do if it is to have any plausibility is to give some account of being human in which we can recognize ourselves. Remember one of the criteria I introduced earlier was this: a worldview needs to provide a framework of meaning in the light of which we can live in the actual world we experience and that makes sense of the experience of ourselves. Stephen Hawking's *A Brief History of Time* is a fascinating read and exhibits an extraordinary intellect.[13] But I am left wondering what light it throws on the phenomenon of ourselves.

I read my first book by a philosopher when I was a teenager. It was Blaise Pascal's *Pensées* ("Thoughts"). It was a marvelous read then and still is. One of Pascal's thoughts stands out:

> Men despise religion. They hate it and are afraid it may be true. The cure for this is first to show that religion is not contrary to reason, but worthy of reverence and respect. Next make it attractive, make good men wish it were true, and then show that it is. *Worthy of reverence because it really understands human nature.* Attractive because it promises true good.[14]

Does Christianity really understand human nature? Pascal thought so. Was he right?

What then does it mean to understand human nature? At the very least this: I need to be able to recognize myself (especially my longings and discontents) in this frame of reference with its touchstone proposition(s). Perhaps a list of questions will help to highlight what needs to be understood.

(1) C. S. Lewis of Narnia fame wrote, "If I find in myself a desire which no experience in this world can satisfy, the most probable explanation is that I was made for another world."[15] If as Lewis suggests we find in ourselves desires that nothing in this world can satisfy, could this be a clue that we are really made for another world beyond this

one? In a letter to a younger aspiring academic, Sheldon Vanauken, Lewis asked:

> If you are really a product of a materialistic universe, how is it you don't feel at home there? Do fish complain of the sea for being wet? Or, if they did, would that fact itself not strongly suggest that they had not always been, or would not always be, purely aquatic creatures? Notice how we are perpetually *surprised* at Time. ("How time flies! Fancy John being grown-up and married! I can hardly believe it!") In Heaven's name, why? Unless, indeed, there is something about us which is *not* temporal."[16]

(2) Why is it that we so hunger for more life—some of us so much so that we are trying to become immortal by melding with the machine to evolve into a new species that can cheat death? As Woody Allen said, "I don't want to achieve immortality through my work; I want to achieve it through not dying."[17] Others hope that at a future date they can be revived from their cryogenic resting places and have the ravages of their terminal illness or ageing reversed.

(3) Why is it that we fall short of our own standards of behavior? What led Nobel prize-winning author Aleksandr Solzhenitsyn in *The Gulag Archipelago* to maintain, "Gradually it was disclosed to me that the line separating good and evil passes not through states, nor between classes, nor between political parties either—but right

through every heart—and through all human hearts"?[18] And what led philosopher Bertrand Russell to lament, "It is in our hearts that evil lies, and it is from our hearts that it must be plucked out"?[19] Do the words of St. Paul resonate with our own moral experience? "I do not understand what I do. For what I want to do I do not do, but what I hate I do. ... For I have the desire to do what is good, but I cannot carry it out" (Rom 7:15, 18b).

(4) Why are we such paradoxical beings? Pascal expressed the paradox in these terms: "What sort of freak then is man! How novel, how monstrous, how chaotic, how paradoxical, how prodigious! Judge of all things, feeble earthworm, repository of truth, sink of doubt and error, glory and refuse of the universe!"[20]

(5) Was Jewish thinker Martin Buber right to describe the human predicament in this vivid contrast: "In the history of the human spirit I distinguish between epochs of habitation and epochs of homelessness. In the former, man lives in the world as in a house, as in a home. In the latter, man lives in the world as in an open field and at times does not even have four pegs with which to set up a tent"?[21] Our postmodern context underlines Buber's point. Some of our contemporaries have given up the search for pegs. For example, Helga Kuhse and Peter Singer maintain: "Since Darwin, we know that we do not exist for any purpose."[22]

(6) What fuels the contemporary quest for spirituality? Is it a growing sense of homelessness? In the swinging '60s Harvey Cox wrote a best seller called *The Secular*

City. He argued that the secularization of Western culture has brought freedom. Traditional religion was now *passé*. But some thirty years later he wrote: "Today it is secularity, not spirituality, that may be headed for extinction."[23] What Cox had not allowed for back in the '60s was a deeply seated human hunger for the transcendent—that is to say, the need to connect with something or someone bigger and more lasting than ourselves. And so what do we now see? The quest for the transcendent currently takes a myriad of forms from interest in the Dalai Lama to Wicca to astrology to scientology to tantric sex. As Bono of U2 sings, we still haven't found what we're looking for.

(7) Is it time to revisit Augustine's famous opening to his *Confessions*, the first Western autobiography? Augustine wrote in the form of a prayer: "because you [God] made us for yourself and our hearts find no peace until they rest in you."[24] It was also Augustine who maintained that although there is truth to be found outside the Bible, there are some premises for thought that can only be found within it.[25] Without these premises for thought we cannot really understand who we are, let alone the wider world in which we live.

3

THE BOOK THAT UNDERSTANDS ME

É MILE CAILLIET WAS born in France early last century and became an eminent scholar, a National Fellow of the French Academy of Sciences. As a young man he sought a book that would understand him. He could not find one so he decided to compile one for himself. Over time he managed to collect quotes from the books he was reading into a leather bound pocket book. A day came when he thought that the book was complete. He sat down under a tree and read it. But as he wrote later: "It carried no strength of persuasion."[26] He was dejected. Around that time his wife—she was Scotch Irish—brought home a Bible in French. Cailliet read a Bible for the first time. At last he had found the book that understood him. Or in Eric Fromm's terms, Cailliet had found a frame of reference. Soon he also found the object of devotion.[27]

So what exactly did Cailliet find in that book that understood him? He found a book, to use philosopher Roger Scruton's words, which was "a hidden door in the scheme of things that opens into another world."[28] In that book, he found a story. But why this story in particular? After all there are many stories out there. The secularist has a story, the Muslim has a story, even Trekkies have a story. Cailliet, however, became convinced that this book tells the *true* story about God, about us and about the world such that he could find his place in it. Of course to mention the word "truth" may cause a smile in some. After all, in these postmodern times, "truth is what your friends let you get away with," as the late postmodern thinker, Richard Rorty, suggested.[29] Truth is a human construct. To claim more is to risk an imperialistic intolerance toward others. (Incidentally this imperialistic tendency is what concerns many postmodern thinkers about the attempt to articulate an encyclopedic worldview.) The funny thing is that when the postmodernist gets the wrong change at the hot dog stand she all of sudden becomes a realist and insists on getting the right change.

So what then is the story that understands me, found in the book that understands me? Novelist Frederick Buechner has said, "The Good Book is a good book."[30] He maintains that despite the diversity of biblical testimonies the essential plot is quite simple: God creates the world, the world gets lost, and God restores the world to its glory. So the big story has sub-stories: stories of creation, stories of lostness, stories of rescue and stories of recovery. Let's look at each in turn.

CREATION

Here's a curious thing: a convinced secularist, Paul Bloom, a Yale professor of psychology and linguistics, thinks that as a species we have all evolved into creationists. Believing in the supernatural is part of human nature. He writes:

"Creationism—and belief in God—is bred in the bone."[31] So what's the explanation? Blind evolution is his answer. Blind evolution makes mistakes and our belief in a creator is one of them. Somehow the enduring human belief that there is more to reality than the senses can detect and more to existence than life in this world needs explaining. These beliefs just won't go away. So instead of denying the cogency of such beliefs, Bloom explains them away as an evolutionary faux pas. Bloom is committed to philosophical naturalism. That is to say, for him, nature is all there is and therefore a closed system of cause and effect. Furthermore, human inquiry must operate on that belief.

A little desperate, methinks. There is another possible explanation as to why these beliefs persist and that even renowned scientists such as Francis S. Collins, the pioneering head of the Human Genome Project, hold them.[32] Maybe these beliefs will not go away because there is truth in them and argument to back them up, despite what Richard Dawkins in his recent book, *The God Delusion*, might think.[33]

The seminal story of creation is found in Genesis 1–2. Whether we read these chapters as literal reportage (and some do), right down to a real tree of life and the tree of the knowledge of good and evil, a talking serpent, etc., or whether we read these chapters as laden with symbolism (and some do)—about real persons, real events, symbolically presented—the point of the story is clear. There is a God who both speaks (reveals) and acts (creates). The creation is not fashioned from pre-existing material by some kind of divine artisan with limited power and skill (a demiurge, to use the ancient Greek expression), nor does it flow out of God's own essence, making all of reality in some sense divine (an emanation). And as for ourselves, in this account we are creatures of a special kind: we have been made in the image of God. We also learn something of the character of this God who creates and reveals. He is interested in creating the good. True, when it comes to human beings, to his special creature made in his image, he sets a limit. In the story there is a certain tree and its fruit is off limits: the tree of the knowledge of good and evil. There is a prohibition. A boundary is set. Yet the first word is not about prohibition but permission. Every other variety of tree is theirs (Adam and Eve's), including that other mysterious tree, the tree of life. Moreover the permitted trees are not only aesthetically pleasing, their fruit is delicious. This God is good and generous. This God is not an enemy of human joy, and this God is not hostile to human sexuality but is its inventor.

Now it is true that we as a species are amenable to chemical analysis. Mostly H_2O, I am afraid. We are of the dust: star dust, the astrophysicists tell us. We are material beings. We like material pizzas, not just the idea of a pizza, to satisfy a very real material hunger. (Make mine pepperoni.) And it is true that we are amenable to biological analysis. We are life and animals, no less. But we are hardly "machines created by our genes," as Richard

Dawkins suggests.[34] Is there a machine that knows that it is machine? We bear the divine image, the Genesis story tells us. That's the difference. We are Godlike in some way. Is it our rationality? Is it our conscience? Is it our need to relate? Is that image not so much in our structure or our relationality but in our role as the highest form of life that is functioning on the Earth? (Indeed, how we function can decide the fate of the planet.) Theologians debate these questions. What is clear is that we are not reducible to mere matter or mere animality or repositories for the selfish gene that needs to replicate itself. We may share an enormous amount genetically with a chimpanzee, but will the chimp ever know it? We do. The creation story is part of the frame of reference, the part that helps us understand our deeply rooted sense of human dignity.

The implications of such an idea of ourselves are legion. That human life is precious is the chief one. Taking human life is a serious moral matter whether in the womb or in law enforcement or in prison or on the battlefield. Nor can human life be reduced in value to the same level as that of other sentient creatures. Philosopher Peter Singer thinks otherwise. On his materialist and naturalistic premises, he argues,

> There will surely be some nonhuman animals whose lives, by any standard, are more valuable than the lives of some humans. A chimpanzee, a dog, or pig, for instance, will have a higher degree of

self-awareness and a greater capacity for meaningful relations with others than a severely retarded infant or someone in state of advanced senility.[35]

But the Christian frame of reference rejects Singer's moral calculus while at the same time respecting the consistency with which Singer follows the logic of his own argument. Another implication is that we are created to work, whether paid or unpaid. In the opening chapter of the Bible, God presents himself as the great worker under the figure of six days on and one day off. (Incidentally how we are to understand the days of Genesis has been a matter of debate from earliest days. When one of the most famous Christian thinkers of all time, Thomas Aquinas, turned his attention to it in the Middle Ages, he simply listed three then-current interpretative possibilities and concluded that however God created the week, it was done in a fitting way.)[36] So too the creature in God's image is a worker. Adam and Eve come before us in the story as workers like God. They are to exercise dominion but not in any kind of mindlessly exploitative way. For the second chapter of the Bible shows us a Neolithic farmer who not only controls the garden but cares for it as well. The health of the environment mattered from the beginning.

The alternative scenario is grim. Writing in the 1960s, Elton Trueblood argued that it was becoming "impossible to sustain certain elements of human dignity, once these had been severed from their cultural roots."[37] He likened his cultural context to that of cut flowers. Flowers once cut from their roots bloom still, at least for a while. But death is coming. In his view, without the acceptance of certain Judeo-Christian ideas about human dignity—such as human beings having been made in the image of God—civilization is in grave danger. On his view, given this cultural trend it is going to become harder and harder to argue convincingly for human value. Peter Singer's views on human dignity quoted earlier provide a case in point.

Neil Postman wittily argues, "The accidental life is not worth living."[38] Human life is not a cosmic joke. There is a design to life that comes from a good and generous God whose word can be trusted. That design calls upon our faith, our rationality, our conscience, and our hunger for lasting relationships. When I was in high school I took a woodworking class. I had no real aptitude for it, but it was compulsory. One lesson stuck with me. If you plane against the grain you will splinter the timber. Go with the grain was the message. If Genesis is right, there is a moral grain to the universe. But do we see the design? So much seems purposeless, even random. If there is a moral grain to the universe why aren't more of us on the same moral page? Historian of ideas Isaiah Berlin insightfully writes of the "crooked timber of humanity."[39] Maybe that timber is not so much crooked as splintered.

That notion brings us to the next part of the story that understands me.

Frank Furedi, a sociology professor at the University of Kent, wrote a witty piece entitled "The Seven Deadly Ills" for *The Spectator*. In it he makes a stunning admission for a secularist. Perhaps we need the Christian category of "sin" after all.

> Once upon a time, there were seven deadly sins. They were called deadly because they lead to spiritual death and therefore damnation. The seven sins were (and are): lust, gluttony, avarice, sloth, anger, envy and pride. Now, all of them, with the exception of pride, have become medical conditions. Pride has become a virtue.[40]

The trouble is, according to Furedi, that to medicalize a moral problem prevents its remedy. He concludes:

> To be honest, as a humanist, I don't much like the idea of sin. But given the choice of being powerless in the face of God or an impotent client of a therapist, I side with the church. Therapeutic definitions of addiction elevate the sense of human powerlessness to a level unimaginable in medieval times. ... Addicts are told that they will never be completely cured. We have recovering sex addicts, recovering religious addicts and recovering alcoholics. No one ever really changes.[41]

Furedi is not opposed to therapy per se. Rather he is alarmed by the way we avoid moral responsibility with a linguistic sleight of hand.

The Bible reader should not be surprised by any of this. Blame-shifting starts as early as Genesis 3 in the tragic turn of events that Augustine termed the fall and Jacques Ellul called the "Rupture." The story of paradise lost is simply told but the resonances are profound. The Creator has a design for life that involves trusting his words of promise and warning. But the man and the woman trust the serpent and their own judgment—that forbidden tree looks so good and the serpent is so plausible. Theologians speculate as to the essence of the Fall. Was it pride? Was it sensuality? Was it rebellion? Was it pride in the male and a failure to take responsibility on the part of the female? Was it unbelief? For the earliest commentary we need to read the Apostle Paul who in his letter to Christians in Rome, the fifth chapter, summed up the falling away as disobedience, a transgression, a trespass, and a sin.

Sin is the great spoiler. Man and woman fall away from God's good and generous design for life. The third chapter of Genesis shows the consequences of sin. The relationship with the Creator is ruptured. Instead of familiarity there is now alienation. The relationship with one another is ruptured. Added to the will to companionship between man and woman there is now the will to dominate the other and shift blame to the other. Even the expression of human sexuality is impacted. Pedophilia, rape, the commodification of women, and pornography are obvious examples. The relationship within ourselves is ruptured. A fear of exposure replaces openness before God: shame has come, and the clothing industry. The relationship with the environment is ruptured. It is thorns, thistles, the sweat of the brow, and back to the dust from which we came. As Pascal gloomily puts it, "The last act is bloody, however fine the rest of the play. They throw earth over your head and it is finished forever."[42]

We are now paradoxical beings. In one of his *pensées*, Pascal wisely contends, "Man's greatness and wretchedness are so evident that the true religion must necessarily teach us that there is in man some great principle of greatness and some great principle of wretchedness."[43] In his book *Faith Seeking Understanding*, Daniel L. Migliore joins the chorus with this observation:

> We human beings are a mystery to ourselves. We are rational and irrational, civilized and savage, capable of deep friendship and murderous hostility, free and in bondage, the pinnacle of creation and its greatest danger. We are Rembrandt and Hitler, Mozart and Stalin, Antigone and Lady Macbeth, Ruth and Jezebel.[44]

Pascal argues that a believable religion "must also account for such amazing contradictions."[45] The Christian doctrine of sin is the part of the frame of reference that does just that.

Many implications follow from the biblical story line at this point. We should not be surprised if there is some ambiguity to our reading the world. There are pointers to God (the good things we experience, such as a beautiful sunset) and pointers away from God (the evils we experience and see, such as famine in Africa). The apostle Paul argues that we live in a groaning creation that itself needs to be set free from the bondage to decay (Rom 8:18–25). That is realism, realism that should carry over to realism about ourselves. We are not "noble savages" who are simply corrupted by civilization, as Jean-Jacques Rousseau thought. The problem is far deeper than the failure to be educated aright. There is a problem endemic to the human heart, which in biblical terms is the core of who we really are. The heart is where our willing, thinking, and feeling have their home. Hard personal experience of his own moral failures taught C. E. M. Joad to rethink his earlier naiveté about human nature. He wrote,

> We on the left were always being disappointed. Disappointed by the refusal of people to be reasonable, by the subservience of intellect to emotion, by the failure of true socialism to arrive, by the behavior of nations and politicians, by the masses' preference of Hollywood to Shakespeare, of Sinatra to Beethoven. Above all, we are disappointed by the recurrent fact of the war. The reason for our

disappointment is that we have rejected the doctrine of original sin.[46]

As we noted earlier, Nobel prize-winning author Aleksandr Solzhenitsyn observed the line of good and evil running through every human heart.

Evil is real—not only moral evils involving the human will, such as the Holocaust, but also natural evils such as a disease amongst wild animals (e.g., Equine flu). The biblical story, however, is far less concerned about the theoretical challenges that such evils pose—a very real interest of the philosopher—as much as the practical one, namely, what is to be done about it. Put another way, the story says very little about the arrival of the problem of evil, that is, how it got here, but much about the survival of the problem of evil, that is, what is being done to address it. And that involves a mysterious promise found in the third chapter of Genesis about the birth of a male child connected to the defeat of the serpent ("a crushed head") and what that defeat will cost him ("a bruised heel").

RESCUE

The realization of the Genesis promise took time. As the story unfolds, God spent centuries preparing a people as the matrix for this realization. The history of Israel in ancient times shows the divine pedagogy at work. Through events, persons, and institutions, God set up the conceptual framework without which we could not have understood how he kept his promise. For example, God rescued Israel from Egyptian slavery through the exodus. A key part of the rescue was the sacrifice of a lamb that averted divine judgment if only people availed themselves of it—an event and a sacrifice that believing Jews celebrate at Passover to this day. God raised up Moses as his agent to put the rescue into effect and to teach his people his design for life, especially the famous Ten Commandments, which centuries later Jesus summed up as love for God and love for neighbor.

The career of Jesus definitively realizes the Genesis promise. He is the agent God sent to accomplish an even greater rescue than ancient Israel experienced. But he was not merely a servant of the divine purpose as Moses was. Instead God sent the Son of his eternal affection. Moreover the problem that Jesus addressed was not political oppression but sin. Sin is that great spoiler that alienates us from the divine life and from one another, and for which we remain accountable before our Creator and liable to his judgment. Still further, the sacrifice offered was not a lamb but that of this Son in willing self-sacrifice. He took the judgment we deserve.

The opening chapter of the Gospel according to John provides a handy presentation of many of these ideas. John starts the story in eternity: "In the beginning was the Word and the Word was with God and the Word was God. He was with God in the beginning" (John 1:1–2). Clearly here is an understanding of God that is complex: "the Word was with God and the Word was God." According to John we are loved with a holy love by a God who is one, yet complex. This God so held the world of men and women in his affections that he gave his unique Son so that whoever entrusts himself or herself to him has everlasting life (John 3:16).

"Trinity" soon became the name to sum up this complexity as the early church thinkers wrestled with the finer details of the nature of God as found in the Christian Bible. Of course, introduce that term "Trinity" and eyes might glaze over. To understand the biblical story, however, requires no less. Once God had taught a people (Israel) that there is only one God and that idols are foolish—one of the great lessons of the Old Testament—then and only then was it safe to unveil the inner reality of who the one God really is: Father, Son, and Holy Spirit—one of the great lessons of the New Testament.

The Trinity is, of course, thoroughly unimaginable. We must, however, distinguish the unimaginable from the inconceivable. That is to say, I cannot form a mental picture of God as Trinity. If I do I find I have a ridiculous mental image of a committee of three meeting on a cloudbank. But to affirm one God in three Persons—Father, Son and Holy Spirit—is not a logical contradiction. It does not parallel attempting to tell the logical story of square circles. Nor is it to assert that there is one God who is three Gods. Now that's a different story; it is not the Christian one.

Moreover, the concept of God as Trinity is immune from that critique as old as Xenophanes (ca. 570–475 BC) and taken up in recent centuries by Feuerbach (1804–72), Marx (1818–83), and Freud (1856–1939). Xenophanes of Colophon argued,

> Yes, and if oxen and horses or lions had hands, and could paint with their hands, and produce works of art as men do, horses would paint the forms of gods like horses, and oxen like oxen, and make their bodies in the image of their several kinds. The Ethiopians make their gods black and snub-nosed; the Thracians say theirs have blue eyes and red hair.[47]

In other words the God/gods in our religious stories worldwide are simply projections of our individual selves or of our societies, just as the ancient Greek gods claimed to live on Mount Olympus. This is a fair critique of much religion in the world today, but of the unimaginable Trinity? I suggest not. The God of the biblical story is no made-up God.

Moreover, if the ultimate reality is the Trinity, then the concept of the Trinity has explanatory power. A longstanding question is: If there is a Creator, why did God create in the first place? Was it out of some divine necessity? After all, a value such as love is a relational value. Love presupposes some other as its object. So did God create out of divine loneliness? This is a serious question to put to any version of theism. Christian theism, however, which is Trinitarian in construal, presents a God who is eternal love on the inside: love among Father, Son, and Holy Spirit. Creation then becomes not an act of divine necessity but an act of divine grace. That is to say, God in creating did what need not have been done. Creation is an overflow of divine largesse.

The story in the Gospel of John does not stay in eternity. This Word is the agent of creation who enters the creation itself, but not without preparation (John 1:3–9). John the Baptist is sent to prepare the way. In fact this Word—still so mysterious—is in the world, the world that he had made. Yet the world rejects his light and life. He even comes to his own (to Israel as its rightful king as well as the whole world's), and the story is the same (John 1:10–11; 19:33–36). However, some do respond and those who trust themselves to him become God's children (John 1:12). Amazingly, the Word becomes flesh (human) in order to reveal the true nature of God as Father (John 1:14). This Word is the Father's Son and has a name, Jesus the Christ (John 1:17).

The Gospel of John is clear that no one has seen God at any time, but it is this Jesus who has made him known (John 1:18). Pascal says, "God being thus hidden, any religion that does not say that God is hidden is not true, and any religion which does not explain why does not instruct."[48] Later in the opening chapter, John the Baptist, the preparer of the way, identifies the Word, the Son, Jesus Christ, as "the Lamb of God who takes away the sin of the world." Our

38

sins hide God's face from us, as it were. This is the answer to Pascal's *why*. In Jesus we find the rescuer and the sacrifice to which the older Scriptures pointed and the one who enables us to turn our faces toward God.

Dorothy Sayers, the detective storywriter and medievalist, wrote in her short piece *The Greatest Drama Ever Staged,* her own summation of the story:

> Whatever game He [God] is playing with creation, He has kept His own rules and played fair. He can exact nothing from man that He has not exacted from Himself. He has Himself gone through the whole of human experience, from the trivial irritations of family life and the cramping restrictions of hard work to the worst horrors of pain, humiliation, defeat, despair and death. ... So that is the outline of the official story—the tale of the time when God was the under-dog and got beaten, when He submitted to the conditions He had laid down and became a man like other men He had made, and the men He made killed Him. This is the dogma we find so dull—this terrifying drama of which God is the victim and hero.[49]

For her, of course, Jesus was no dead hero. (This is the case likewise for the writer of the Gospel of John.) As she wrote in an essay on the Easter story, "God did not abolish the fact of evil: He transformed it. He did not stop the crucifixion: He rose from the dead."[50]

Incidentally the story of the cross shows us why all stories cannot be equally true. The cross is the symbol of Christianity worldwide. Islam, however—to take one example—claims that Jesus did not die on the cross.[51] On the Islamic view it is impossible that Allah would allow such a great prophet to perish in that way. Someone has clearly got the story wrong. If I may update an observation of the philosopher E. S. Brightman: A universe in which both Christianity [Brightman said, Roman Catholicism] and Islam [Brightman said, Christian Science] were true would be a madhouse. The principle of non-contradiction needs to be observed. "A" cannot be non-"A" at both the same time and in the same respect. A typewriter cannot be blue all over and red all over at the same time and in the same respect. For make no mistake: both Christianity and Islam claim that their foundational stories are not merely useful fictions, or, to use Plato's expression, "a noble lie."

Indeed there is no reason to embrace either the story of Jesus or that of Muhammad unless the seminal story speaks of what happened in real space and real time. And to look no further than the Gospel of John, there we find the writer makes the claim that "we have seen his glory," and in another place writes of the reality of Jesus' death: "The man who saw it [blood and water flow from Jesus' side] has given testimony, and his testimony is true" (John 1:14; compare 19:35).

40 What follows from taking this narrative seriously, rooted as it is in a real coming and a real cross? In brief,

on this view—as with the idea of creation in the divine image—we matter. We are not cosmic orphans. We are not the chance products of time and chance. We are not subject to a blind fate. Nor are we subject to a cruel deity. King Lear thought that we were: "As flies to wanton boys are we to th'gods, / They kill us for their sport."[52] Nor has the Creator abandoned us. Our experiences of evils may challenge such claims. Writer Arthur Koestler was wrong to suggest that God has left the phone off the hook when it comes to human misery. If the biblical story of the incarnation (the Word became flesh) is to be believed, then God has come among us under the conditions of real human life. It is a long-standing debate among theologians as to whether God can suffer. Older theology argued *no* (e.g., Thomas Aquinas). Generally speaking, more recent theologians say *yes* (e.g., Jürgen Moltmann). Be that as it may, the incarnation at the very least shows us that God knows what it is to weep a human tear as Jesus did at the tomb of his friend Lazarus (John 11:35) and to die a human death (John 19:30). On the Christian view, evil is being addressed, and the universe is not indifferent to the wrong we do.

The story of the cross also shows that the problematic of human wrongdoing cannot be solved by anything less than a radical remedy. Education can ameliorate the human predicament but it is naïve to think that it alone can bring in utopia. To think so is to fall into what might be termed "the Socratic fallacy." This is the notion that if one knows the truth one will do it. Historically speaking, some highly educated folk have proved to be moral monsters. The Nazi era comes to mind. Joseph Goebbels, the Nazi propaganda minister, had an earned doctorate in eighteenth-century romantic literature from the University of Heidelberg. In our present context the Socratic fallacy can be wedded to another. This fallacy could usefully be described as "the technocratic fallacy." Cultural analyst Os Guinness sums up the attitude this way: "A breakthrough a day keeps disaster at bay." If only it were that simple. The scientific enterprise is a most worthy one and a singularly great achievement of the human spirit. However, there is a scientism that displays a confidence in science—albeit narrowly construed—that goes well beyond what the scientific method can accomplish. This "ism" is not so much science as ideology. Scientism is one of the more unfortunate expressions of modernity (the Enlightenment). A concern for argument and evidence is one of the more fortunate. The problem lies not in science per se or technology per se but in us who wield it. For example, consider the double-edged sword of nuclear energy. We have the nuclear bomb and nuclear medicine. We can exterminate a city or heal a cancer sufferer.

In sum: the supreme rescue story of the Bible constitutes that part of the frame of reference that helps us to understand why Jesus is so special. Further, it helps me grasp how the goodness and love of God can be believed in a world such as our own with its beauties and its terrors, its delights and its dangers. And still further it helps me to comprehend how I can find peace when I become acutely aware of my true moral status before a holy, loving God who will not overlook human wrongdoing forever, including my own. Yet God has provided through the coming and cross of Christ what I cannot do for myself: he has provided in Jesus a mediator and reconciler. Jesus lived an other-person-centered life in his humanity that should be true of each one of us but isn't. In other words, he lived the divine design for human life: love for God and neighbor. The value of his faithfulness to the divine design can be put to our account if we avail ourselves of it. He also died the death we deserve because of our wrongdoing so that we might not face God's judgment if we avail ourselves of its value. He makes an extraordinary exchange possible. Martin Luther drew an analogy for that exchange by writing of a marriage. The riches of Christ become that of his bride the church and the great debts of the bride are swallowed up by those riches.[53] And this Jesus is returning. Creation awaits its restoration and its King. There are limits, however, to the divine patience.

RESTORATION

In today's world, so also in Jesus' day: there are those who give up hope of a better world beyond this one. When a teleological (goal-oriented) perspective on history is abandoned then hedonism or apathy or despair or nihilism follows. E. M. B. Green gives an example of the first three from inscriptions on ancient tombs. One tomb has: "I was nothing; I am nothing; so you who are still alive, eat, drink, and be merry." This is hedonism (pleasure is the only good). Another shows apathy: "Once I had no existence; now I have none. I am not aware of it. It does not concern me." His next example found on yet another tomb reads: "Charidas, what is below? Deep darkness. But what of the paths upward? All a lie. ... Then we are lost."[54] Here is despair of a chilling kind. In Shakespeare's magnificent play *Macbeth*, there is a scene in which Macbeth learns of his wife's death, which leads him to lament:

> To-morrow, and to-morrow, and to-morrow,
> Creeps in this petty pace from day to day,
> To the last syllable of recorded time;
> And all our yesterdays have lighted fools
> The way to dusty death. Out, out, brief candle!
> Life's but a walking shadow, a poor player,
> That struts and frets his hour upon the stage,
> And then is heard no more. *It is a tale*
> *Told by an idiot, full of sound and fury,*
> *Signifying nothing.*[55]

This is the nihilistic conclusion.

Others both then and now have hungered for immortality. There are those who hope that cryogenics will mean that at some later date, well after their death, they can live again and be cured of whatever killed them in the first place. Still others hope that their science will enable the next evolutionary leap. Robo-sapiens or transhumans are coming on this view—human and machine melded into a new species that can cheat death. Millions of dollars are being spent on this quest at some of the most prestigious universities in the West. Some governments are attracted to the quest because of its military potential: the enhanced or augmented soldier of the future.[56] To some, the science fiction film *RoboCop* represents the hoped-for future.

A characteristic of the biblical story is its hopefulness. Hope, after all, is one of the great virtues alongside faith and love. Peter in his first letter writes of Christians who have been born again to a living hope (1 Pet 1:3–5). This hopefulness is founded on an astounding historical event, the resurrection of Jesus Christ from the dead and his return. The King is returning—and I am not talking about Elvis. The head of the serpent has been crushed as the ancient promise of Genesis suggested. Yet not all has played out. According to Peter in his second letter, time has been allowed for humankind to hear and respond to the divine plan. Oscar Cullmann captured the scenario vividly by drawing an analogy between the New Testament understanding of time and the way the war in Europe against Hitler unfolded.[57] D-Day in 1944—so remarkably presented in Steven Spielberg's "Saving Private Ryan" and also in his "Band of Brothers"—was the turning point in that theater of World War II. That day, June 6, "marked the beginning of the victory of the Allies in Europe."[58] However, it wasn't until V-E Day the following year, May 8, 1945, that armistice was declared after Germany surrendered.[59] We live, as it were between the divine D-Day and V-E Day.

Importantly this concept of hope is not to be confused with the weak secular version found today. In the latter version hope is equivalent to a wish. I hope that the stock market becomes bullish again. But with the stock market there are no guarantees. By contrast, as St. Paul preached to the Athenian intelligentsia so long ago: "For he [God] has set a day when he will judge the world with justice by the man he has appointed [Jesus]. He has given proof of this to all men by raising him from the dead" (Acts 17:31). St. Paul would have little time for the postmodern view that I heard expressed recently—that if you believe in resurrection you will be resurrected, if you believe in reincarnation you will be reincarnated, if you believe that there is no life beyond the grave then there will be no life beyond the grave. Everybody is right. No one has got it wrong. In contrast, Paul argued in one of his letters that if he had got it wrong about the resurrection then he was to be pitied more than anyone because there was then no answer for his plight and he had misrepresented God by declaring falsely that God had raised Jesus from the dead (1 Cor 15:12–19).

Christian hopefulness also engenders a particular perspective on human history. Unlike some other great religions of the world, especially from the East, Christians are roadies not wheelies. Let me explain. Lesslie Newbigin sees a key divide between those who believe that the human story will be endlessly repeated like a wheel turning on its axis but not actually going anywhere (reincarnation and eternal recurrence) and those who see human history as a road.[60] He reached this conclusion after spending many years in India dialoguing with Hindu scholars. A road has a beginning, a middle, and an end. The biblical story too has a beginning, middle, and an end. It starts in a garden in the first book of the Bible, Genesis, and ends the human story in a city in the last book of the Bible, Revelation. In the middle is the coming and cross and resurrection of Christ. The journey is from the old heavens and earth to a new heavens and earth. Evil is no more, death is no more, tears are no more, mourning is no more. The universe is at peace; it is characterized by *shalom*, by God-given well-being.

Technically, the book that understands me presents a comedy—not comedy in the Simpsons' sense, but in the literary one. The movement is from harmony through descent into tragic disharmony before the restoration of a richer harmony than the beginning.[61] The great poet Dante understood this in his magnificent work, *The Divine Comedy*. It ends on the note of "The love of God that moves the sun and the other stars."[62]

The implications of the king's returning are legion. To begin with, the horizon to our life is not the next paycheck or vacation break—at least not in ultimate terms. We are to live as the classic phrase put it: *sub specie aeternitatis* ("under the aspect of eternity"). Immanuel Kant argued that one of the great questions we can ask is, "What may I hope?"[63] The Bible's answer is plain: the coming again of Christ. This frame of reference keeps the Christian from

47

both naïve utopianism and dyspeptic pessimism. The quintessential expression of the latter is found in Bertrand Russell's famous essay *A Free Man's Worship*:

> Such, in outline, but even more purposeless, more void of meaning, is the world which Science presents for my belief. Amid such, if anywhere, our ideals henceforward must find a home. That man is the product of causes which had no prevision of the end they were achieving; that his origins, his growth, his hopes and fears, his loves and beliefs, are but the outcome of accidental collocations of atoms; that no fire, no heroism, no intensity of thought and feeling, can preserve an individual life beyond the grave; that all the labour of the ages, all the devotion, all the inspiration, all the noonday brightness of human genius, are destined to extinction in the vast death of the solar system, and that the whole temple of Man's achievement must inevitably be buried beneath the debris of a universe in ruins—all these things, if not quite beyond dispute, are yet so nearly certain, that no philosophy which rejects them can hope to stand. *Only within the scaffolding of these truths, only on the firm foundation of unyielding despair, can the soul's habitation henceforth be safely built.*[64]

Some fifty years later another secularist, Lord Blackham, adds to this pessimism: "The most drastic objection to humanism is that it is too bad to be true. The world is one vast tomb if human lives are ephemeral and human life itself doomed to ultimate extinction."[65] Some contemporary scientific theory about the future reinforces both Lord Russell's and Lord Blackham's gloomy conclusions. Although the universe is expanding post big bang, there is a day coming on which gravity will win out and then comes the big crunch and the end of all things human.

Now someone might say that if the story is to be believed then why doesn't its chief character turn up not incognito but in full divine display now? Then we would all believe. I wonder if the questioner really understands what he or she is asking for. To use Francis Fukyama's phrase, we would be at "the end of history" as we know it. It is a kindness of God's that the end is still coming. There is a window of opportunity for us to change our minds about our lives and to embrace the story. For the final great event before a renewed heavens and earth is the last judgment. On that occasion there will be no doubts as to whose universe this is, and by then our allegiances will be set.

4

DESCRIBING:
IS IT ENOUGH?

W HEN IT COMES to the claim to know, philosophy introduces an important distinction. Philosopher Bertrand Russell in his famous book *The Problems of Philosophy* distinguishes knowledge by description from knowledge by acquaintance.[66] Knowledge by description is propositional. I know that Abraham Lincoln was the President during the Civil War years. I can read about it in books and look at the old photos. I live in Illinois, his home state, which means that I can easily visit the Lincoln museum in Springfield. In contrast, knowledge by acquaintance is personal familiarity. The French language likewise has a nice distinction between two words for knowing. *Savoir* is used for facts or knowing by heart or even knowing how to do something. "I know that Paris is the most famous city in France." *Connaître* is used for people and places known by acquaintance. *Connaître* is always followed by a direct object. In fact, I know Paris. I've been there and taken the boat tour on the Seine with my wife and daughter. A frame of reference or worldview is about *connaître*, not *savoir*, whether religious or scientific. As philosopher Roger Scruton says: "Our knowledge of God is a matter of personal acquaintance, which cannot be conveyed in the language of science."[67] For that reason I suspect that ultimately there is radical insufficiency about worldview thinking alone. For *savoir* alone is not enough to satisfy the deep places of the heart.

DOES CHRISTIANITY
HAVE A WORLDVIEW?

The short answer is yes and no. Christianity has a worldview (technically, theism) but isn't a worldview. As for the *yes*, there is a cluster of touchstone propositions at the heart of an intellectual account of Christianity: propositions about the Creator, the creation, the fall, the rescue, and the restoration. Moreover as we have seen earlier, this frame of reference not only has explanatory power—that is, it makes sense of our experience—it also raises significant questions about naturalism, secularism, modernity, postmodern relativism, naïve romanticism, utopianism, nihilism, pessimism, Islam, Hinduism, and the transhuman project as alternative stories. Frames of reference have both a positive and a negative function. They attempt to explain and to exclude. Even a frame of reference such as a thorough-going pluralism, which argues any frame of reference is viable, has trouble inviting to the table frames of reference that are expressed in absolutist terms. "Absolutely no absolutes!" as the ironic saying goes.

As for the *no*, historically the term Christianity was used first to describe the religion of people who had given their allegiance to Jesus rather than to Caesar. Caesar was described as Lord (*kyrios*) and savior (*sōtēr*) and news of his birthday or accession was labeled "good news" or "gospel" (*euanggelion*). These are the very words used by early Christians to refer to Jesus and the message about him. He is the true Lord, the true Savior, and the message about him is good news indeed. The implied political challenge to the empire by these words may be one reason that to confess to be a Christian could be punished by death, as governor Pliny's letter to the Emperor Trajan shows (early second century). True Christians, he found, were prepared to suffer for that label. Furthermore, they refused to curse Christ and worship Caesar instead.[68]

The first recorded use of the word Christianity that I know is found in the letters of Ignatius, Bishop of Antioch, as he made his way under guard to his martyrdom early in the second century. He wrote a letter to Christians in Magnesia in which he contrasted Christianity with Judaism. In other words he was contrasting not one philosophy or worldview over against another (e.g., Stoicism versus Christianity), but one religion over against another.[69] Or to use Eric Fromm's language once more: he was contrasting objects of devotion, not frames of reference.

Christianity is first of all news of a person and his significance and not views about the world. Yet it has very definite views about the world, as we have seen, with big organizing ideas for thought such as God, Christ, creation, fall, rescue, and restoration. To put it in Eric Fromm's terms, Christianity does provide a frame of reference.

ASSESSING FRAMES OF
REFERENCE OR WORLDVIEWS

At this point someone might respond, "OK, so Christians have a worldview. Well, so what? There is more than one worldview out there. Why settle for the Christian one?" A fair comment, for it raises the question of how we are to do quality control on worldview candidates. Let me develop further the two important criteria mentioned earlier. These criteria apply to frames of references and to worldviews—whether we have in mind the more modest existential worldview that I equate with a frame of reference or the encyclopedic that attempts to cover everything.

The first criterion is whether the frame of reference is thinkable. That is to say, when articulated does it tell a logical story in two senses of the word? Is the story internally consistent or does it contradict itself? That's one sense. If we allow the contradictory, then anything follows. Imagine if I tried to tell someone that Christ was killed by crucifixion and that he lived to a ripe old age and had a family before passing away in his sleep. The other sense is the need for a coherent story. The elements in the story need to illuminate one another. The sub-stories of creation, fall, rescue, and restoration throw light on one another. The story of the Christ's cross outside the walls of Jerusalem and the story of how Jack Daniels makes whisky down in Tennessee do not cohere in any obvious way. A frame of reference or worldview—at whatever level of sophistication—needs to be logically adequate.

The second criterion is livability. If I believe and embrace a particular frame of reference, am I able to live as though it were true to my experience of the world? Or will the living of life betray its inadequacy? Bertrand Russell tells the story of a woman who had discovered a philosophical view known as solipsism. Solipsism maintains that the only consciousness to be found is your own. She wrote to Russell wondering why more people weren't solipsists. In other words, she didn't live as though solipsism were true to fact (i.e., the actual state of affairs). We might call this criterion that of lived or existential adequacy.

Now some might say, "Wait! Christians don't always live as though their frame of reference is true." Sadly that can be the case. The question is whether the Christian frame of reference actually explains such existential inconsistency, the difference between the espoused and the operational. It does. Christians are forgiven but not yet perfected people. This does not excuse hypocrisy. Because so much of the New Testament was written to smarten Christians up, there is realism in its pages about human behavior this side of the ultimate restoration. For example, in the last book of the Bible, Revelation, there are several letters to various churches (Rev 2–3). Five of the seven churches receive criticism for wrong belief or wrong behavior. Only two receive unreserved commendation. This realism is what is to be expected if the Christian frame of reference with its idea of the fall and of a complete restoration to come is taken seriously.

AN INVITATION

As we have noted, an explanatory perspective on life is one thing, but the living of it is another. The danger of worldview talk is that it remains just that: talk, talk, talk. Some Christian thinkers have noted this danger. In his own inimitable style, Søren Kierkegaard imagined this scenario. When Christians die and go to heaven they will be confronted by two doors. One will have this sign on it, "Heaven." The other will have, "Lecture on Heaven." He thought most Christians would go to the lecture.[70]

Let's look at it this way. Imagine that you are living in a condo listening to the sounds of a party in the street below. You analyze the live music. You think that it is pretty good. In fact, you are drawn to the music and the evident joy of the people in the street below. Those people really do seem to be enjoying themselves. You speculate as to why such gaiety. Someone below sees you up there and waves to you, beckoning you to come down and join the festival. She says the party is moving on and that you are welcome to come. She also adds that the party is in honor of a great one whom they are all waiting for. The invitation is there, but what will you do? Will you leave the balcony, take the elevator and step onto the road? Or is it all too easy to remain a spectator? The condo is comfortable, the air conditioning is on and you have cable. So why investigate further? Put another way, the trouble is that worldview thinking can be like sharpening a knife but never cutting anything.

Remember too what Fromm said about not only having the human need for a frame of reference, but also an object of devotion. The party is celebrating someone on whose story hangs the destiny of us all. It is beyond our scope to say more about the central who and what of the story—Jesus himself. According to the Gospel of John, "Jesus did many other things as well. If every one of them were written down, I suppose that even the whole world would not have room for the books that would be written" (John 21:25). He also wrote that the purpose of his book—selective though it might be—was that the reader may believe that Jesus is the Christ and that by so believing may have life in his name (John 20:31). The life that John writes about is not merely biological, but life that not even physical death can undo—what he calls "eternal life." As Gregory A. Clark suggests: "The best case for Christianity, then, is not the coherence and comprehensiveness of its worldview. Jesus himself is the most persuasive case for Christianity."[71]

5

UNDERSTANDING THE BOOK THAT UNDERSTANDS ME

N OW SOMEONE MIGHT say, "Well, that's only your interpretation!" Others read the story differently. Indeed they do. So then how about you do some reading for yourself? Get yourself a Bible in a modern translation. There are some good ones around: for example, the *New International Version*, the *English Standard Version*, and the *New Revised Standard Version*. Start at the start (Gen 1–3) and then go straight to the end (Rev 21–22).

Genesis 1–3 introduces God as Creator, creation, humanity in the divine image, the fall, and the foundational promise concerning the defeat of evil. Revelation 21–22 takes us to the end of the story. Here we read of the new heavens and the new earth, the restoration of creation, and the absence of evil. Ask yourself how the story goes from that beginning in Genesis 1–3 to that ending in Revelation 21–22. Next read about God's call to Abraham in Genesis 12:1–3 and how God rescues Abraham's descendants in Exodus 1–3 and identifies himself to Moses, one of those descendants, by name as the great "I am who I am." As the subsequent history of Israel unfolds, God shows himself by his deeds to be the God who both saves and judges. Move on to the prophet Isaiah—one of the highpoints of the Old Testament—and the promise of someone to come. This someone would put things right, but at great personal cost (Isa 52:12–53:12). That promised someone is Jesus.

The Gospel according to John is good for that latter part of the story. In John 1–3 we learn of the Word who is God the Son and the Messiah of Israel. He is the Lamb of God who takes away the sin of the world. We also learn of how God's love for the world led to the gift of the Son's coming and his cross. Next read John 11–12. In these chapters we see Jesus breaking death's hold over his friend Lazarus and the necessity for Christ's sacrifice. Unless the seed dies, there is no fruit. Then read John 18–20. These chapters narrate how Jesus the Lamb of God bears away the sins of the world and overcomes death.

Finally, for a sweeping picture of the human predicament and the divine response to it, read Paul's Letter to the Romans 1–5. Romans 1–3 is a sobering analysis of the human predicament climaxing in the claim that whoever you are you have fallen short of God's glorious intention for humankind. Romans 4–5 tells of how Jesus' life, death, and resurrection are the divine answer to the human predicament, and that the answer is accessed by a faith like that of Abraham's. Finally, add in Romans 8 for good measure. Here is a unique passage in the writing of the ancient world. Matter has a future in God's plans. Creation will be set free from its bondage to decay to become the context for the revealing of God's glorious children. Those who belong to Christ experience no condemnation from God and will experience no separation from the love of Christ.

Read with sympathy and imagination. Some people read the Bible very woodenly. Let me illustrate. Suppose we work together and this one morning I come to work in a great panic. I tell you that America's longstanding ally Britain has been invaded. There is mayhem everywhere. Historic buildings are burning. You are puzzled. You had watched *CNN* that very morning before work and there was not a hint of any of this. So you ask me how I know all this. I reply that I read it in the morning's newspaper. In fact I inform you of the invading general's name, Hagar the Horrible. "You fool!" you say, "He's a cartoon character." I find some people read the Bible with less sophistication than they read their newspaper. In reading the newspaper they sort out the cartoon from the editorial from the weather report from the advertisement from the TV program guide from the feature article. In other words they recognize that even a newspaper exhibits many different kinds of communication. So when you read the Bible, be prepared to encounter a variety of literary types of expression: parable and fable, poetry and prophecy, history and proverb, letters and genealogies—to name some. Be prepared for surprises. God has imagination.

Acknowledgments

T HE SERIES Questions for Restless Minds is produced by the Christ on Campus Initiative, under the stewardship of the editorial board of D. A. Carson (senior editor), Douglas Sweeney, Graham Cole, Dana Harris, Thomas McCall, Geoffrey Fulkerson, and Scott Manetsch. The editorial board recognizes with gratitude the many outstanding evangelical authors who have contributed to this series, as well as the sponsorship of Trinity Evangelical Divinity School (Deerfield, Illinois), and the financial support of the MAC Foundation and the Carl F. H. Henry Center for Theological Understanding. The editors also wish to thank Christopher Gow, who created the study questions accompanying each book, and Todd Hains, our editor at Lexham Press. May God alone receive the glory for this endeavor!

Study Guide Questions

1. In the opening section, Cole gives two criteria for an acceptable "frame of reference"—what are they? How are they different?

2. How would you summarize the Bible's story in four points?

3. Why do you think God became incarnate?

4. What are some implications that follow from the Biblical story; if the Biblical story is true, so what?

5. What is the Socratic fallacy? Why is it a fallacy?

6. Can you think of any other examples of things that people place their hope in for salvation that cannot ultimately provide help?

7. How does Cole respond to the objection that Christians often don't live in a manner that is consistent with their frame of reference?

For Further Reading

Naugle, David K. *Worldview: The History of a Concept.* Eerdmans, 2002.

> Fills an important gap in worldview scholarship by showing how the concept has been used by a myriad of thinkers past and present. Thorough and scholarly.

Pascal, Blaise, *Pensées.* Translated by A. J. Krailsheimer. Penguin, 1972.

> Pascal was a many-sided genius and a deep Christian thinker. *Pensées* is a classic in philosophical writing, especially his famous wager argument for the existence of God.

Sire, James W. *The Universe Next Door: A Basic Worldview Catalog.* 4th ed. IVP, 2004.

> Skillfully examines a plethora of worldviews: Christian Theism, Deism, Naturalism, Nihilism, Existentialism, Eastern Pantheistic Monism, the

New Age, and Postmodernism. Written with clarity and verve.

———. *Naming the Elephant: Worldview as a Concept.* IVP, 2004.

Goes deeper and tackles the meta-questions that concern the theoretical underpinnings of worldview thinking. Interacts with Naugle's discussion and explores "Worldviews as a Tool for Analysis." An intentional companion to *The Universe Next Door*.

Trueblood, Elton. *A Place to Stand.* Harper & Row, 1969.

Written after teaching philosophy for fifty years. Takes up the claim of Archimedes (the inventor of the fulcrum) that if he had a place to stand he could move the world. Argues that Christ as he comes before us in the Gospels is that place to stand. A good read for those who like the autobiographical approach.

Wolters, Albert M. *Creation Regained: Biblical Basics for a Reformational Worldview.* Eerdmans, 1985.

A slim volume but filled with great insight into a Christian approach to worldview thinking in terms of the interplay of creation, fall, and restoration.

Notes

1. Eric Fromm, *Beyond the Chains of Illusion: My Encounter with Marx and Freud* (Simon and Schuster, 1962), 3–11.

2. Quoted in Neil Postman, "Science and the Story that We Need," *First Things* 69 (January 1997): 29, emphasis mine.

3. Postman, "Science and the Story," 30.

4. For an excellent study of the concept of a worldview, see David K. Naugle, *Worldview: The History of a Concept* (Eerdmans, 2002).

5. Quoted in Richard Symonds, "The South Stoke Festival of Thought," *Philosophy Pathways* 32 (2002), http://klempner.freeshell.org/newsletter/issue32.html.

6. Naugle, *Worldview: The History of a Concept*, 58–59.

7. Jean-François Lyotard, *The Postmodern Condition: A Report on Knowledge,* trans. Brian Massumi and Geoff Bennington (University of Minnesota, 1984).

8. William H. Halverson, *A Concise Introduction to Philosophy*, 4th ed. (McGraw Hill, 1981), 414–15.

9. Halverson, *A Concise Introduction*, 9–10 (his emphases).

10. John Warwick Montgomery, *The Suicide of Christian Theology* (Bethany Fellowship, 1970), 122.

11. Frank Morison, *Who Moved the Stone?* (Faber and Faber, 1944).

12. According to J. Gresham Machen, "The Bible offers news—not reflection on the old, but tidings of something new; not something that can be deduced or something that can be discovered, but something that has happened; not philosophy, but history; not exhortation, but a gospel" ("History and Faith," https://www.readmachen.com/article/1915/history-and-faith).

13. Stephen W. Hawking, *A Brief History of Time: From the Big Bang to Black Holes* (Bantam, 1988).

14. Blaise Pascal, *Pensées,* trans. A. J. Krailsheimer (Penguin, 1972), 34 (emphasis added).

15. C. S. Lewis, *Mere Christianity* (Collins, 1958), 118.

16. Quoted in Sheldon Vanauken, *A Severe Mercy* (HarperOne, 1987), 93 (emphasis his).

17. Quoted in Paul Bloom, "Is God an Accident?" *Atlantic Monthly* 296/5 (December 2005): 105.

18. Aleksandr I. Solzhenitsyn, *The Gulag Archipelago, 1918–1956: An Experiment in Literary Investigation,* vol. 2, trans. Thomas P. Whitney (Harper & Row, 1974), 615.

19. Quoted in "Bertrand Arthur William Russell," http://www.giga-usa.com/quotes/authors /bertrand_arthur_russell_a001.htm.

20. Pascal, *Pensées*, 64.

21. Martin Buber, *Between Man and Man* (Fontana, 1961), 157.

22. Helga Kuhse and Peter Singer, eds., *Bioethics: An Anthology* (Blackwell, 2001), 4.

23. Harvey Cox, "The Warring Visions of the Religious Right," *Atlantic Monthly* (November 1995): 59–68.

24. Augustine, *Confessions*, trans. R.S. Pine-Coffin (Penguin, 1977), 21.

25. Augustine, "De Doctrina Christiana," in *Augustine on Education* (Henry Regner, 1969), 359.

26. Émile Cailliet, *Journey into Light* (Eerdmans, 1968), 16. Cailliet illustrates the conflict between naturalism and non-naturalism that Halverson addresses. Cailliet describes his early education as "naturalistic to the core" (11).

27. Fromm argues that a religion consists not only in a frame of reference but also an object of devotion. See Erich Fromm, *Psychoanalysis and Religion* (Yale University, 1970), 21.

28. Roger Scruton, *Gentle Regrets: Thoughts from Life* (Continuum, 2006), 1.

29. Quoted in Thomas Riggins, "Remembering Richard Rorty 1931–2007," https://leninlives.blogspot

.com/2007/06/remembering-richard-rorty-1931-2007.html.

30. Frederick Buechner, "The Good Book as a Good Book," in *The Clown in the Belfry: Writings on Faith and Fiction* (HarperSanFrancisco, 1992), 44.

31. Bloom, "Is God an Accident?" 110–11.

32. Francis S. Collins, *The Language of God: A Scientist Presents Evidence for Belief* (Free Press, 2007).

33. Richard Dawkins, *The God Delusion* (Houghton Mifflin, 2006). Also see the spirited reply by Alister E. McGrath and Joanna C. McGrath, *The Dawkins Delusion? Atheist Fundamentalism and the Denial of the Divine* (IVP, 2007).

34. Richard Dawkins, *The Selfish Gene*, 2nd ed. (Oxford University, 1989), 2.

35. Peter Singer, *Animal Liberation: A New Ethics for Our Treatment of Animals* (Jonathan Cape, 1976), 19. For a critique of Singer's views see Gordon R. Preece, ed., *Rethinking Peter Singer: A Christian Critique* (IVP, 2002).

36. Thomas Aquinas, *Summa Theologica*, part 1a, question 74.

37. Elton Trueblood, *A Place to Stand* (Harper & Row, 1969), 14–15. In fact Trueblood had been arguing this thesis from the 1940s: see his *The Predicament of Modern Man* (Harper & Row, 1944), 59–60.

38. Postman, "Science and the Story That We Need," 31.

39. Isaiah Berlin, *The Crooked Timber of Humanity: Chapters in the History of Ideas*, ed. Henry Hardy (Knopf, 1991). Berlin is indebted to Kant for the crooked timber image.

40. Frank Furedi, "Making a Virtue of Vice," *The Spectator* (January 12, 2002); repr., "The Seven Deadly Sins," *The Weekend Australian* (February 2–3, 2002): 26.

41. Furedi, "Making a Virtue of Vice," 27.

42. Pascal, *Pensées*, 82.

43. Pascal, *Pensées*, 76.

44. Daniel L. Migliore, *Faith Seeking Understanding: An Introduction to Christian Theology*, 2nd ed. (Eerdmans, 2004), 139.

45. Pascal, *Pensées*, 76.

46. Quoted in Roy Clements, *Masterplan: How God Makes Sense of Our World* (Inter-Varsity Press, 1994), 43–44.

47. Quoted in Rex Warner, *The Greek Philosophers* (Mentor, 1962), 24.

48. Pascal, *Pensées*, 103.

49. Dorothy L. Sayers, *The Greatest Drama Ever Staged* (Hodder and Stoughton, 1938), 9–10.

50. Sayers, *The Greatest Drama*, 43.

51. *The Koran*, 2nd ed., trans. N. J. Dawood (Penguin, 1980), Sura: "Women," 4.158. 382–83.

52. William Shakespeare, *King Lear*, 4.1.36–37. References are to act, scene, and line.

53. Martin Luther, "The Freedom of the Christian Man," in *Martin Luther: Selections from His Writings*, ed. John Dillenberger (Doubleday Anchor, 1961), 60.

54. Quoted in E. M. B. Green, *2 Peter and Jude* (Inter-Varsity Press, 1974), 139. I am indebted to Green for these examples, but I have modernized the English.

55. William Shakespeare, *Macbeth*, 5.5.19–28 (emphasis added).

56. Ellen Ullmann, "Programming the Post-Human: Computer Science Redefines 'Life,' " *Harper's Magazine* (October 2002): 60–70.

57. See David H. Wallace, "Oscar Cullmann," in *Creative Minds in Contemporary Theology: A Guidebook to the Principal Teachings of Karl Barth, G. C. Berkouwer, Dietrich Bonhoeffer, Emil Brunner, Rudolf Bultmann, Oscar Cullmann, James Denney, C. H. Dodd., Herman Dooyeweerd, P. T. Forsyth, Charles Gore, Reinhold Niebuhr, Pierre Teilhard De Chardin, and Paul Tillich*, ed. Philip Edgcumbe Hughes (Eerdmans, 1973), 169.

58. Joseph F. Kett, E. D. Hirsch Jr., James Trefil, *The New Dictionary of Cultural Literacy: What Every American Needs to Know*, completely revised and updated ed. (Houghton Mifflin, 2002), 224. The term "D-Day" is used by the military to refer to the day when a strategic initiative is to begin. See

Rebecca N. Ferguson, *The Handy History Answer Book* (Visible Ink, 2000), 158.

59. V-E stands for Victory in Europe.

60. Lesslie Newbigin, *The Finality of Christ* (John Knox, 1969), 65–67.

61. See Leland Ryken, *The Literature of the Bible* (Zondervan, 1980), 22–23.

62. Quoted in E. L. Mascall, *The Christian Universe* (Darton, Longman and Todd, 1967), 55.

63. Immanuel Kant, *Critique of Pure Reason,* trans. John Meiklejohn (George Bell and Sons, 1901) 583.

64. Bertrand Russell, "A Free Man's Worship," https://users.drew.edu/~jlenz/br-ml-ch3.html (emphasis added).

65. H. J. Blackham, *Objections to Humanism* (Lippincott, 1963), 105.

66. Bertrand Russell, *The Problems of Philosophy* (Oxford University Press, 1978), 25–32.

67. Scruton, *Gentle Regrets: Thoughts from Life*, 234.

68. Quoted in Henry S. Bettenson, ed., *Documents of the Christian Church*, 2nd ed. (Oxford University Press, 1967), 3.

69. Ignatius of Antioch, "Letter to the Magnesians," in *Early Christian Writings: The Apostolic Fathers*, ed. Maxwell Staniforth (Penguin, 1972), 90.

70. Quoted in Robert K. Johnston, *God's Wider Presence: Reconsidering General Revelation* (Baker Academic, 2014), 1.

71. Gregory A. Clark, "The Nature of Conversion: How the Rhetoric of Worldview Philosophy Can Betray Evangelicals," in *Evangelicals and Liberals in Conversation*, ed. Timothy R. Phillips and Dennis Okholm (IVP, 1996), 218.

LEXHAM PRESS

QUESTIONS FOR RESTLESS MINDS

CLARIFYING ANSWERS ON QUESTIONS FOR RESTLESS MINDS

Series Editor: D. A. Carson

The Questions for Restless Minds series applies God's word to today's issues. Each short book faces tough questions honestly and clearly, so you can think wisely, act with conviction, and become more like Christ.

Learn more at lexhampress.com/questions